THE WAR SHE WON

A Poetry Collection of Survival, Strength, and Healing

ISABEL BARRETT

© 2025 Isabel Barrett

All rights reserved.

No part of this publication may be reproduced, distributed, or transmitted in any form or by any means—electronic, mechanical, photocopying, recording, or otherwise—without the prior written permission of the publisher, except in the case of brief quotations used in critical reviews or permitted by copyright law.

First edition. Printed in the United States.

For rights, permissions, or inquiries, contact:
info@seedsoflightpublishing.com

Published by
Seeds of Light Publishing LLC
www.SeedsOfLightPublishing.com

Interior & Cover Design by HMDPublishing.com

"When you pass through the waters, I will be with you; and through the rivers, they shall not overwhelm you. When you walk through fire, you shall not be burned, and the flame shall not consume you."
– Isaiah 43:2

For every woman who found strength in her scars,
For every woman still in the trenches,
For every woman finding her voice—
This is for you.
May you always know you are seen, you are heard, and you are not alone.
Your story matters. Your healing matters. Your victory is coming.
For the hearts still on the journey—your strength inspired this book.

Preface

This book is for you. For the ones who have endured, the ones still healing, and the ones who refuse to stay silent. I know the weight of your pain, the battle scars that tell a story many will never understand. But I also know this: **you are unshaken, and you are not alone.**

I never set out to write a book about survival. I never imagined that my own pain, my own battles, and my own moments of breaking would one day find their way into these pages. Yet, here they are—not as wounds, but as words. Not as sorrow, but as strength.

Writing this book was more than a journey—it was a **declaration**. Each poem was written not just for my healing, but for yours. May you find strength, courage, and restoration in these pages.

This collection of poetry is a reflection of survival, resilience, and healing. Each poem was written for the woman who is reclaiming her voice, her strength, and her light. May these words remind you that you are more than what happened to you—you are the **war she won.**

Whether you are still in the storm or standing in the sunlight of your healing, may this book remind you that you are never alone, that your strength is greater than you know, and that your story—every part of it—deserves to be told.

This is *The War She Won*—not just my war, but yours too. And together, **we stand in victory**.

With love and strength

Isabel Barrett

Contents

Introduction: Opening Letters to Survivors 8
    Ink & Tears..11

01. The Fire She Walked Through......................... 13
    I Rise, Unbroken 17
    She Didn't Break 19
    The Hands That Saved Me 21
    A Letter to My Younger Self............................. 23
    Scars and Stories 25
    No Longer Afraid 27
    Reflection & Journaling.................................. 29

02. The Rebirth of a Woman 31
    Shedding the Old Me......................................35
    From Ashes to Wings 37
    The First Time I Chose Me................................39
    Healing Takes Time.......................................41
    No More Apologies 43
    This Woman Will Not Bow 45
    The War at Night...47
    Reflection & Journaling..................................49

03. The Power of Motherhood............................. 51
    A Mother's Hands 55
    She is Watching 57
    The Silent Strength of Mothers 59
    A Love That Never Ends 61
    To the Mother Who Feels Invisible 63
    Legacy...65
    For the Mother Who Carries the Weight of Two 67
    Reflection & Journaling..................................69

04. The Silence & The Storm, The War No One Sees........ 71
    The Silence That Chokes..................................75
    The War Inside.. 77
    Nightmares & Echoes 79
    Sleepless & Unshaken 81
    It Comes Without Warning............................... 82
    Loving Me Won't Be Easy..................................85
    Reflection & Journaling................................. 87

05. Worthy of Love...................................... 89
    Love Does Not Break You 93
    I Am Not Asking for Too Much.............................95
    I Waited for the Right Love 97
    He Sees My Strength 99
    If He Makes You Feel Small 101
    A Love That Stays 103

      When Love Feels Impossible 105
      Reflection & Journaling. 107

06. Finding Her Voice Again, Healing Through Words 109
      No Longer a Whisper 113
      From Whisper to War Song 115
      I Used to Apologize for My Story. 117
      This is My Reclamation. 119
      Ink & Tears. 121
      The Power of Speaking 123
      Not Broken, Becoming 125
      Reflection & Journaling. 127

07. The Light She Found in God's Grace & Guidance 129
      Through the Storm, I Remained. 133
      The Fire Within 135
      She Became the Storm. 137
      The Light in Her Hands 139
      After the Storm 141
      I Remind Myself— 143
      Reflection & Journaling. 145

08. The War She Won. 147
      Written in Ink and Tears 151
      Every Scar a Victory 153
      Strength in His Name 155
      The War Was Never Hers to Carry. 157
      Reflection & Journaling. 159

09. Unapologetically Me 161
      Take the Pen Back 165
      Unapologetically Me 167
      No More Apologies 169
      Loving Me Won't Be Easy. 171
      Reflection & Journaling. 173

10. A Legacy of Strength & Restoration 175
      For the Ones Still in the Trenches 178
      Strength in Her Own Name 181
      Restoration 183
      Decades Later, It Still Hurts 184
      Legacy. 187
      Reflection & Journaling. 189

Acknowledgments 191
Survivor Resources & Organizations 193
Afterword 195
Anchored in Truth: Scriptures for Strength & Restoration . . 197

Introduction: Opening Letters to Survivors

This book is not just a collection of words.
It is **a voice**—yours, mine, and the ones who have stayed silent for too long.

I know what it's like to carry a story that feels too heavy to tell.
To hold memories that no one else sees.
To live with pain that lingers long after the wounds have faded.

Maybe you've spent years pretending you're okay.
Maybe you've smiled through moments where your soul felt shattered.
Maybe you've convinced yourself that no one would understand—
so you **say nothing.**

But I want you to know this:

You are **not alone.**
Your story **matters.**
Your pain **is real—but so is your healing.**

This book is for every woman who has survived.
For the ones still **in the trenches** and the ones who have climbed out.
For the ones who have found their voice
and the ones who are still learning to speak.

You do not have to carry this alone.
There is **hope**—real, unshaken, undeniable hope.
There is **healing**—not just survival, but **restoration.**
There is a God who sees you, who never abandoned you,

who has been holding you **even on the nights you thought you were completely alone.**

This is your story, too.
And no matter where you are in your journey—**you are not broken, you are not ruined, you are not beyond saving.**

You are **unbreakable.**

There is power in a woman's voice.
There is healing in her story.
There is strength in her survival.

This book is for every woman who has fought battles in silence.
For the ones who have risen from the ashes of pain.
For the mothers who pour love into their children, even when they feel empty themselves.
For the women who refuse to settle for less than they deserve.

May these poems be a reminder that you are not alone. That you are seen. That you are worthy.

You are unbreakable.

Ink & Tears

Every word on the page
is ink mixed with tears,
a release of memories,
a surrender of pain.

Writing is my healing,
turning darkness into light,
pouring secrets onto paper,
until they no longer own me.

Through ink and tears,
I find freedom,
one word at a time.

The Fire She Walked Through

The Fire She Walked Through: An Introduction

Survival is never gentle—it's forged in fire, shaped through struggle, and defined by the battles we endure. This chapter honors every woman who has faced flames meant to consume her, yet emerged stronger, wiser, and more resilient. Within these pages, scars become testimonies, pain transforms into power, and survival is celebrated not as a mere act of endurance, but as an unshakable declaration of strength.

I Rise, Unbroken

I have walked through fire,
felt the rage of the storm,
the breaking of bones that were never meant to heal,
the silence after betrayal so deafening
I swore the earth swallowed me whole.

I have known the sharp edge of sorrow,
the hollow ache of nights that refused to end,
the way pain makes a home in your chest
until you forget how to breathe without it.

But still, I rise.
Not as the woman they buried,
not as the girl who once begged to be saved,
but as the wildfire they never saw coming.

I rise with the fury of a thousand suns,
with the strength of ancestors who refused to bow.
I am not what happened to me—
I am what survived.

She Didn't Break

They thought she would shatter,
thought the weight of the world
would crush her fragile bones.

But they didn't know—
this woman was carved from the spine of mountains,
molded by storms,
forged in the fire of every war she survived.

She did not break.
She bent like the willow,
folded but never fell,
swayed in the hurricane but never surrendered.

And when the storm finally grew tired,
when the world thought she was nothing but dust,
she stood taller than ever before—
unshaken, unbreakable, reborn.

The Hands That Saved Me

I reached for love in all the wrong places.
Found it in hands that held me too tight,
in arms that crushed instead of cradled.
I called it love,
but love was never meant to leave bruises.

I searched in shadows,
whispered prayers into pillows soaked with grief,
pleaded for something greater than my own strength—
until He answered.

The hands that once trembled in fear
now lift in praise.
The heart that once begged for love
now beats with a fire that cannot be extinguished.

The world told me I was not enough,
but my God whispered back—
You are mine.

And that was all I needed to hear.

A Letter to My Younger Self

Dear girl with the shattered heart,
I know how heavy your sorrow is,
how you stare at the ceiling and wonder if it's worth it,
if the pain will ever end,
if you are destined to always feel this lost.

Let me tell you something—

One day, you will wake up,
and the grief that suffocated you
will have loosened its grip.
One day, you will look in the mirror
and recognize the fire in your eyes again.

And the world will try to tell you that you are broken,
that you are damaged goods,
that no one loves a girl who has been through the storm.

But let me remind you—
only warriors survive the fire.

So keep going, my love.
God is not done with you yet. He still has a plan.

Scars and Stories

Every scar tells a story,
a whisper of war etched into my skin,
a roadmap of battles fought and won.

They ask me if I regret the pain,
if I wish I had lived a softer life,
if I dream of a version of myself
untouched by fire.

And I tell them no.

Because these scars?
They are my history, my proof,
the ink of my survival story
written in flesh.

I do not wear them in shame.
I wear them in power.
Because I did not just live through the pain—
I conquered it.

No Longer Afraid

I used to fear the night.
The shadows creeping, the voices whispering—
telling me I was too weak, too broken,
too lost to ever find my way again.

But I have seen the dark,
and I have walked through it.

Now, I do not tremble.
Now, I run into the night with open arms,
because I have learned—
the darkness holds no power over the ones
who became their own light.

I am no longer afraid.
I do not fear the storm,
because I am the storm.

Reflection & Journaling

What is one battle you've walked through that made you stronger?

_____
_____
_____
_____

If you could go back in time, what would you tell yourself during your hardest moments?

_____
_____
_____
_____

What is one piece of your story that you've been afraid to tell? How would it feel to set it free?

_____
_____
_____
_____

The Rebirth of a Woman

The Rebirth of a Woman: An Introduction

Shedding the past is never gentle. It is raw, uncomfortable, and at times, it feels like breaking all over again. But rebirth is not about staying whole—it is about letting go of everything that was never meant to stay.

She once clung to the version of herself that apologized too often, that dimmed her light to make others comfortable, that carried pain in silence because she thought that was strength. But no more.

She is rising now. She is stepping into the woman she was always meant to be. And though the past whispers, though the scars still remember—she does not turn back.

Because she is not who she was. She is who she is becoming. And that is something beautiful.

Shedding the Old Me

I no longer fit in the skin of the woman I used to be.
She was afraid, fragile, and unsure.
She apologized for taking up space,
softened her voice so the world wouldn't hear her.

But I have outgrown the fears she carried.
I have stripped off the weight of expectation,
peeled away the layers of who they told me to be,
and beneath it, I have found someone unbreakable.

She is not small.
She is not silent.
She is not sorry.

I am new.
I am reborn.
I am unafraid to bloom.

From Ashes to Wings

They buried me in doubt,
layer after layer, until I forgot the sun.
They told me I was too much, too wild, too untamed.
So I folded,
took up less space,
let the ashes of their words settle over me.

But fire does not destroy—
it transforms.

One day, the embers of my soul stirred,
and I rose, unapologetic, untamed,
turning my past into power.
I am not the woman who was buried—
I am the woman who emerged.

A new creation.

The First Time I Chose Me

The first time I said no,
my heart pounded in my chest.
The first time I put myself first,
they called me selfish.

But I had spent too long
pouring from an empty cup,
swallowing my own needs
so the world could stay comfortable.

The first time I chose me,
I felt like I was betraying someone.
But I wasn't.

I was returning home to myself.

Now I see—choosing me was never wrong.

Healing Takes Time

Healing is not linear.
Some days, you move mountains.
Others, you can barely lift your head from the pillow.

There are days when the past whispers,
when old wounds feel fresh again,
when progress feels like an illusion.

But healing is not about perfection—
it is about persistence.

Even when it is slow,
even when it is painful,
even when you cannot see the change—
healing is happening.

You are healing.
Even now.

No More Apologies

I do not owe the world an apology
for being too loud,

too quiet,

too much,

too little.

I am simply, wholly, beautifully—me.

This Woman Will Not Bow

I have bent, but I will not break.
I have stumbled, but I will not fall.
I have suffered, but I will not stay wounded.
I rise, because I was made for more.

The War at Night

They tell me to rest,
but they don't know what the night holds.

When the world grows quiet,
my mind grows loud.
The darkness does not bring peace—
it brings memories,
woven into the sheets,
curled into the silence,
waiting.

I close my eyes,
but sleep does not come easy.
The past does not believe in locked doors.
It moves through the cracks,
settles into my ribs,
presses against my chest
until breathing feels like a battle.

The blankets feel heavy,
like the weight of everything I swore I let go of.
I flip the pillow,
as if a cooler side
will erase the fire beneath my skin.

I count breaths.
I count heartbeats.
I count the hours until the sun rises,
because daylight is the only thing
that makes it easier to exist.

Reflection & Journaling

What is one part of yourself that you are ready to let go of?

_____
_____
_____
_____

When was the first time you truly chose yourself?

_____
_____
_____
_____

If you could describe your rebirth in one sentence, what would it be?

_____
_____
_____
_____

The Power of Motherhood

The Power of Motherhood: An Introduction

Motherhood is not soft hands and lullabies alone. It is sacrifice, it is resilience, it is waking up before dawn and carrying a weight no one else can see. It is standing strong when little eyes are watching, teaching love even when your own heart aches, and pouring from a cup that sometimes feels empty.

She did not know the kind of strength she carried until she held life in her arms. She did not realize she was a warrior until she fought for the ones who needed her most.

This chapter is for the mothers who break cycles, who raise daughters to be bold and sons to be kind, who fight silent battles and still choose love. Because motherhood is not just nurturing—it is power.

A Mother's Hands

These hands have held, healed, and wiped away tears.
They have braided hair, buttoned tiny shirts,
packed lunches, and carried dreams.

These hands have worked tirelessly in love.
They have held a sleeping child through the night,
gripped steering wheels with tired fingers,
and wiped away silent tears no one saw.

These are not just hands—
they are the foundation of generations.

She is Watching

My daughter watches how I love myself.
So I will teach her to stand tall,
to embrace her voice,
to never shrink for anyone.

She watches how I speak,
so I choose my words with kindness.
She watches how I love,
so I love without fear.

She is learning strength by watching me,
so I will show her
what it means to be unshaken.

The Silent Strength of Mothers

Mothers do not always roar.
Their strength is in the steady hands
that hold, that heal, that never waver.

Their love is in the sleepless nights,
the whispered prayers,
the quiet sacrifices no one sees.

Mothers are not fragile—
they are the backbone of resilience,
the steady force that keeps the world standing.

A Love That Never Ends

From the moment she was placed in my arms,
I knew—this love would never break,
never fade, never falter.

To the Mother Who Feels Invisible

You are seen.
You are loved.
You are the heartbeat of your home,
the force that keeps it together.

Legacy

The strength in my bones,
I pass to her.
The wisdom in my words,
I teach her.
The love in my soul,
I leave with her.

For the Mother Who Carries the Weight of Two

I do not heal just for me.
I heal because little eyes are watching.
Because my strength is their first lesson.

There are days when the past knocks on my door,
when the weight of everything I have endured
feels like too much to carry.

But I have learned—
I do not walk alone.

My child does not know the wars I have fought,
but they know the way my hands never shake
when I hold them close.

They do not know the nights I could not breathe,
but they know that in my arms, they are safe.

They do not know the battles I lost,
but they will grow up knowing that I won.

Because I refuse to pass down
anything but strength.

Reflection & Journaling

How has motherhood (or mother figures in your life) shaped your strength?

_____
_____
_____
_____

If you could leave one message for the next generation, what would it be?

_____
_____
_____
_____

What does a strong mother look like to you?

_____
_____
_____
_____

The Silence & The Storm, The War No One Sees

The Silence & The Storm. The War No One Sees: An Introduction

Not all battles leave visible scars. Some storms rage silently within, unseen by others, hidden behind forced smiles and whispered reassurances that "everything's okay." In this chapter, we step courageously into the shadows, shedding light on the invisible wars many fight every day—the ones marked by anxiety, sleepless nights, and relentless echoes of the past. Here, we give voice to the unspoken, acknowledge the unseen, and remind ourselves and each other that healing begins when silence is broken

The Silence That Chokes

I want to tell you,
but the words do not come.

I want to say,
"I'm not fine,"
"The past lingers,"
"Some nights, my mind does not let me rest."
But my voice locks up before the truth can reach air.

You ask what's wrong,
and I say, *"I'm just tired."*
Because it's easier to blame exhaustion
than admit I am carrying something heavier than sleep.

I wish I could pull the weight from my chest
and place it in your hands
so you could understand
why some nights, I stare at the ceiling
instead of sleeping beside you.

I wish I could tell you
why I tense when you reach for me too fast,
why I pull away when your love is safe.

It is not you—
It is the pieces of the past
that still take up space in my body.

The War Inside

There is a war inside me,
one the world never sees.
A quiet chaos,
an endless storm beneath the calm,
a battlefield behind a smile
that hides more than it reveals.

Every sunrise, I arm myself,
ready for a battle no one sees,
against shadows I cannot name,
and fears that speak in whispers.

Yet every day, I rise again.
Not because the war is over,
but because I am stronger
than the battles fought in silence.

Nightmares & Echoes

Nightmares visit me like old friends,
uninvited but familiar,
haunting hallways in my mind.
They linger at my bedside,
waiting to remind me
of moments I begged to forget.

But in the echo of every scream
is proof that I survived,
that the past cannot silence me.

My dreams might be haunted,
but I am awake now,
stronger than the nightmares
that try to claim me.

Sleepless & Unshaken

Sleep eludes me,
but strength never does.

Even when shadows chase rest away,
when anxiety dances behind closed eyelids,
I remain awake—unshaken,
my breath steady,
my heart determined.

The night may hold memories,
but morning brings new strength.

I am sleepless,
but never defeated.

It Comes Without Warning

It comes without warning.

A sound, a scent, a touch—
and suddenly, I am not here anymore.
I am back where it happened,
back where I swore I'd never be again.

I tell myself, *"This is now. That was then."*
But my body does not know the difference.
My hands shake.
My breath fights to find air.
My heart beats so fast
it forgets its own rhythm.

I try to move,
but my feet are frozen in place,
trapped in a past
that still has its grip on me.

Someone speaks.
I hear them,
but the words are swallowed
by the sound of my own panic.

"Breathe."
"Come back."
"You're safe now."

But in this moment,
I do not feel safe.
I do not feel here.

I feel like I am drowning
in something no one else can see.

And that is the worst part of all—
no one sees this war but me.

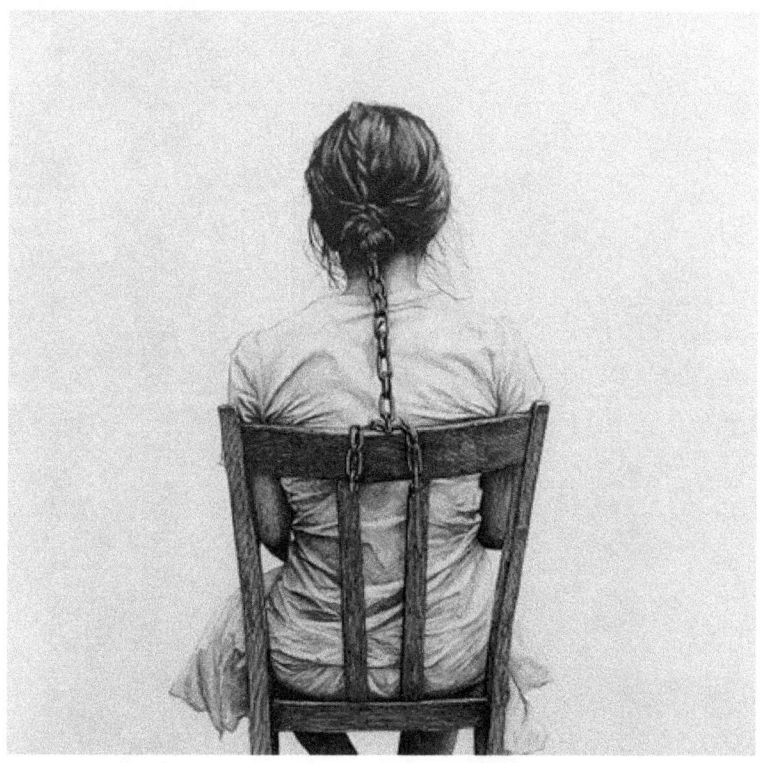

Loving Me Won't Be Easy

Loving me won't be easy.

Some nights, I will pull away,
not because I do not love you,
but because I have spent years
learning how to protect myself
from the kind of love that was never real.

I have been kissed by lips
that turned promises into empty air.
I have been held by hands
that claimed to love me
but only left bruises—
some you could see,
some you never will.

So when I flinch at your touch,
when I stare into the distance
instead of into your eyes,
please know—
I am trying to believe that love
can be safe,
that hands can be gentle,
that I do not have to keep my guard up
to survive.

If you stay,
be patient with the parts of me
that are still learning
how to be held
without bracing for impact.

Reflection & Journaling

What do you wish the world understood about invisible battles?

_____
_____
_____
_____

What does healing look like for you? Describe it in detail.

_____
_____
_____
_____

Worthy of Love

Worthy of Love: An Introduction

After facing storms that left scars, embracing the idea of love can feel impossible, almost frightening. Yet, love was never meant to diminish or hurt—it was meant to uplift, empower, and heal. In this chapter, we reclaim our belief in love that honors, respects, and cherishes. We recognize our worth, no longer settling for less, and learn that true love never asks us to become smaller. Here, we find the courage to believe that we are, and have always been, worthy of genuine, unwavering love.

Love Does Not Break You

Real love does not silence your voice.
It does not shrink your dreams.
Real love expands you—
it lifts, not limits.

I Am Not Asking for Too Much

I only ask for what I give:
kindness, respect, devotion.
If that is too much,
then they are too little for me.

I Waited for the Right Love

I did not settle for hands that could not hold me,
for hearts that did not honor me.
I waited—
and now love is soft, steady, sure.

He Sees My Strength

He does not fear my fire,
nor does he try to tame it.
He simply warms himself
by its glow.

If He Makes You Feel Small

If he makes you feel like you must shrink
to fit beside him—
he is not the one.

A Love That Stays

Not love that fades,
not love that breaks,
but love that stays—
that is the love I choose.

When Love Feels Impossible

Loving me will not be easy.

I have lived through too much,
felt too many things that were not love
but wore its disguise.

I have been promised safety
by those who never meant to keep me safe.
I have given my trust
to hands that were not gentle.

So when I pull away,
when I hesitate at your kindness,
please understand—
this is not me pushing you away.
This is me learning that love
is not supposed to be a battlefield.

I have built walls
not because I do not want to let you in,
but because I do not know what to do
with a love that does not come with pain.

Be patient with me.
Be steady.
Be real.
Because the only way I will ever believe
that love is safe—
is if you show me.

Reflection & Journaling

Describe what healthy, genuine love looks and feels like to you. What qualities and behaviors make you feel truly cherished?

_____
_____
_____
_____

Think of a moment when you felt deeply respected and loved. What was different about that relationship or moment compared to others?

_____
_____
_____
_____

List three non-negotiables you will now look for in your relationships to honor your worth.

_____
_____
_____
_____

Finding Her Voice Again, Healing Through Words

Finding Her Voice Again, Healing Through Words: An Introduction

Words hold profound power—the power to heal, to transform, and to reclaim. For those who've been silenced, discovering the strength of their own voice becomes a journey of profound healing. In this chapter, we reclaim our voices, turning whispers into declarations, scars into stories, and pain into power. Here, we learn to speak unapologetically, boldly, and freely—each word a step closer to full restoration.

No Longer a Whisper

I used to whisper

my story

like an apology.

Now, I tell it like a

War Song

From Whisper to War Song

My voice began as a whisper,
afraid to disturb the stillness,
trapped beneath the weight
of words unspoken,
truths untold.

But a whisper could not carry
the power of my story,
so I learned to shout.
Each word became louder,
stronger,
more sure of its right to be heard.

Now my voice sings
a song of survival,
a war cry echoing freedom.
From whisper to war song—
my truth can never be silenced again.

I Used to Apologize for My Story

I used to apologize for my scars,
as though healing was something
to hide, to make smaller,
to diminish into silence.

I spoke in hushed tones,
ashamed to burden others
with my truth.
But silence kept me trapped
in the very past I longed to escape.

Now, I speak boldly,
unapologetic, proud—
because my story isn't a burden,
it's a beacon.

This is My Reclamation

This is my reclamation—
the moment I choose my truth
over their comfort.

I reclaim every word,
every memory,
every broken piece,
transforming trauma
into a story of strength,
of renewal, of power.

I am not who they said I was.
I am who I choose to become.
This voice is mine,
and I reclaim it now,
forever.

Ink & Tears

Every word on the page
is ink mixed with tears,
a release of memories,
a surrender of pain.

Writing is my healing,
turning darkness into light,
pouring secrets onto paper,
until they no longer own me.

Through ink and tears,
I find freedom,
one word at a time.

The Power of Speaking

Words have power,
and mine no longer tremble.
My voice breaks through silence,
carrying truth with strength,
shattering chains built by fear.

The power of speaking
is the power of healing,
of reclaiming,
of rebuilding.

I speak,
and with every word,
I become whole again.

Not Broken, Becoming

They said I was broken,
but broken things can heal,
can grow,
can transform.

I am not broken—
I am becoming.

I am building myself
from fragments,
each piece stronger,
each scar proof
of battles won,
of healing embraced.

Reflection & Journaling

Write a poem about the moment you realized you were healing.

_____
_____
_____
_____

Write a letter to your past self, reminding her of her strength.

_____
_____
_____
_____

The Light She Found in God's Grace & Guidance

The Light She Found in God's Grace & Guidance: An Introduction

There comes a moment after the storm when darkness finally yields to dawn, and clarity replaces chaos. In this sacred stillness, we recognize the grace that carried us, the unseen strength that guided our steps when we couldn't see the way forward. This chapter is an invitation to step into the light, embracing the healing warmth of grace, redemption, and the gentle power of surrender. Here, we remember that even in our darkest moments, we were never alone.

Through the Storm, I Remained

I have lived inside

Storms that should have

drowned me.

But I learned how to

breathe underwater

I have walked through fire

meant to **consume me.**

But now I carry the

Flame.

The Fire Within

I once feared the fire,
thought it would consume me,
turn me to ashes,
leave me unrecognizable.

But I have learned—
fire does not always destroy.
Sometimes, it refines.
Sometimes, it awakens
what was always meant to burn brightly.

Now, the fire within me
is not something to fear,
but something to honor.
It is not destruction—
it is rebirth.

She Became the Storm

They told her to be gentle,
to shrink herself into softness,
to be rain instead of thunder.

But she learned that storms
are not just chaos,
they are cleansing,
they are fierce,
they make way for new beginnings.

She did not become smaller.
She did not silence her winds.
She did not tame the lightning inside her.

She became the storm,
and in doing so,
she became free.

The Light in Her Hands

She searched for light in others,
in places that could not hold her glow,
in hands too unsteady to carry something so radiant.

But she was never without light—
it had always been there,
resting in her palms,
waiting to be recognized.

Now, she no longer searches.
She simply opens her hands
and lets the light shine.

After the Storm

It comes like a storm—
violent, sudden, unforgiving.
It takes over my body,
my mind, my breath,
until I am nothing
but panic wrapped in skin.

But like all storms,
this one will pass.

I have weathered these before.
I have felt the shaking hands,
the racing heart,
the dizzying fear
that tries to convince me
this moment will never end.

But it does end.
It always does.

And when it does,
I am still here.
Still breathing.
Still standing.
Still whole.

The storm does not own me.
The past does not own me.

I take one breath.
Then another.

I Remind Myself—

I remind myself—
I am here.
I am safe.
I am free.

No longer bound
by the chains of yesterday.
No longer drowning
in the weight of what was.

God did not bring me through fire
just to leave me in the smoke.
He parted seas,
He moved mountains,
He carried me
when I could not stand.

So I stand now,
rooted, strong, unshaken.
I am here.
I am safe.
I am free.

Reflection & Journaling

Write about a moment when you realized God's grace was guiding you.

_____
_____
_____
_____

How has faith or inner strength helped you through a storm in your life?

_____
_____
_____
_____

The War She Won

The War She Won: An Introduction

Victory is more than just surviving—it's thriving in spite of every obstacle, scar, and setback. It's standing tall not because we never fell, but because each fall taught us resilience, each wound became wisdom, and each battle shaped us into warriors. This chapter celebrates the journey of victory, healing, and true restoration. It's a tribute to every woman who has risen above, let go of burdens that were never hers to carry, and discovered a strength she never imagined she possessed.

Written in Ink and Tears

every chapter of my life

has been written in

Ink and Tears

but this page is different-

this one is filled with

Light

Every Scar a Victory

They called them scars,
but I see them as markers,
proof of the battles I've fought,
and the wars I've won.

Each one a lesson,
each one a testament to the fire I walked through,
and the strength that carried me forward.

I do not hide them.
I wear them boldly,
not as wounds, but as victories.

Strength in His Name

She searched for strength in borrowed voices,
in names spoken over her,
in validation that never stayed.

But when she called upon Him,
her strength was no longer her own.

She stood, not by her power, but by His.

She was never meant to carry it alone.

She was never the source, but always the vessel.

Her name was known in heaven,
and that was enough.

The War Was Never Hers to Carry

She carried battles that weren't hers,
held the weight of wounds that were never meant to be hers to heal.

She mistook survival for responsibility,
thought that strength meant holding it all.

But strength is knowing when to put the burden down.

She does not have to carry it anymore.

She is free.

Reflection & Journaling

If you could offer one piece of wisdom to someone still fighting their battle, what would it be, and why?

_____

_____

_____

_____

Describe a moment when you truly felt victorious and free from past burdens. How did this moment change your perspective?

_____

_____

_____

_____

Unapologetically Me

Unapologetically Me:
An Introduction

There comes a point in every healing journey when we finally choose ourselves—not apologetically, not hesitantly, but boldly and unconditionally. This chapter celebrates that moment of reclaiming. It's about refusing to apologize for existing fully, beautifully, and authentically. Here, we embrace our truths, accept our imperfections, and declare with unwavering confidence: this is who I am, and I will never shrink again.

Take the Pen Back

They tried to write me out of

My own story.

But I took the Pen back.

Now every word is

mine.

Unapologetically Me

I do not owe anyone my suffering.
I do not owe anyone my silence.

I have spent too many years
swallowing my own voice
so others could feel comfortable,
so my pain would not disturb
the peace of those who never knew war.

Not anymore.

Now, I choose me.
I choose morning walks in soft sunlight.
I choose books that remind me of my worth.
I choose to say no without guilt
and yes without fear.

I choose soft blankets,
strong coffee,
deep rest,
and the kind of joy
that makes my heart feel like home again.

They told me self-care was selfish.
I tell them self-care is survival.

No More Apologies

I will not shrink to fit spaces
that were never meant to hold me.
I will not swallow my words
to make silence more comfortable.

I have spent too long apologizing
for the fire in my spirit,
for the way my voice carries,
for the strength in my stance.

No more apologies.
No more bending
for those who fear my fullness.
I am not here to be small.
I am here to be seen.

Loving Me Won't Be Easy

Loving me won't be easy.

I have known the weight of loss,
the sting of promises left unkept,
the ache of arms that held me too tightly,
and hands that let me go too soon.

I have built walls,
not to keep love out,
but to see who is willing
to climb them with me.

Loving me will take patience.
It will take gentleness,
and steady hands
that do not flinch
at the sight of old wounds.

But if you stay,
you will see—
I am not a woman meant to be saved,
I am a woman meant to be understood.

Reflection & Journaling

What does it mean to live unapologetically?

_____

_____

_____

_____

What parts of yourself have you previously apologized for or hidden away? How does embracing these parts fully change your journey toward healing and authenticity?

_____

_____

_____

_____

Describe the life you envision when you stop apologizing for who you truly are. How will your relationships, dreams, and daily life transform?

_____

_____

_____

_____

A Legacy of Strength
& Restoration

A Legacy of Strength & Restoration: An Introduction

Healing doesn't end when the wounds close; it continues through the strength we pass forward, the courage we inspire, and the restoration we embody. This final chapter is about more than personal triumph—it's about the lasting legacy we leave behind. It's a testament to resilience, to the transformative power of restoration, and to the strength found not only in surviving, but in truly thriving. Here, we celebrate the journey completed and the path of hope laid out for those who follow.

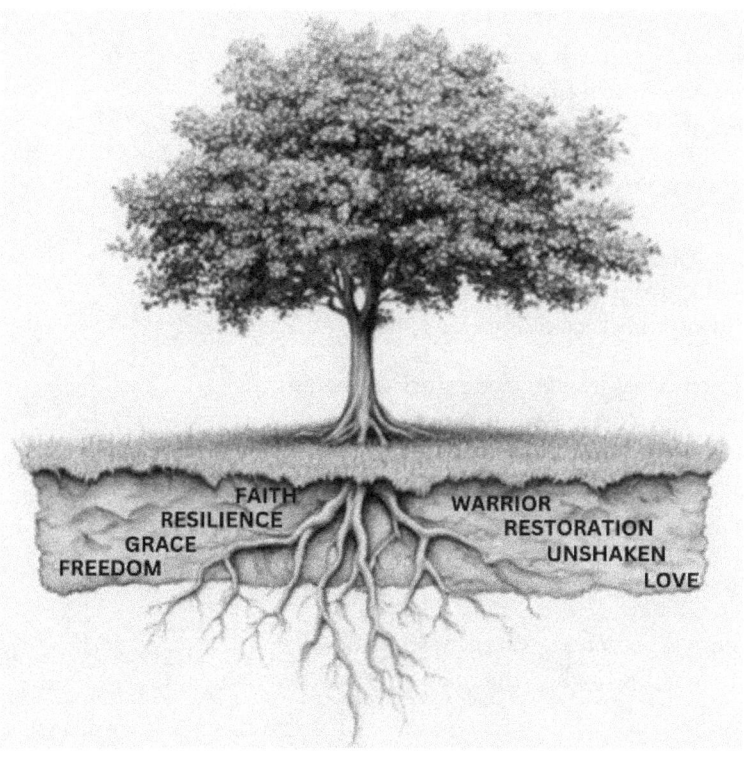

For the Ones Still in the Trenches

I see you.
The woman who never speaks of what was done to her.
The one who fakes a smile
because the truth is too heavy to carry in conversation.

I see the way your hands shake
when someone gets too close,
the way you laugh at things
that do not feel funny
because it is easier than crying.

I see the way you wake up
more exhausted than when you fell asleep.
The way you stare at ceilings,
waiting for morning,
praying for peace that never comes.

I know what it's like to be stuck in the past
while the world keeps moving forward.
To live in a body that still flinches,
still remembers, still carries the weight
of hands that were not kind.

But I promise you—

There is something on the other side of this.
There is a day when the memories will not own you.

When the past will no longer be a prison,
but a story you survived.

I know it's hard to believe,
but you will not be in the trenches forever.

You are not alone in this.
You never were.
And one day, you will see—
God has been reaching for you all along.

Strength in Her Own Name

She was never meant to carry their burdens,
to hold the weight of their expectations,
to shrink herself so they could stand taller.

She spent years trying to fit,
trying to be small enough,
soft enough,
silent enough.

But strength does not live in silence.
Power does not bow to comfort.
She speaks her name now,
and it holds weight,
not because they gave it power,
but because she did.

She is strong
because she chose to be.
Because she refused to be anything less.
Because she knows now—
her name was always enough.

Restoration

For too long, I have been in survival mode.
Bracing for impact.
Expecting pain before it comes.
Living like peace was something
meant for others,
but never for me.

But He said,
"I did not just call you to survive—
I called you to LIVE."

And suddenly, I realized
I was not made to exist in the aftermath
of my pain forever.

I was not made to flinch at love,
to question joy,
to fear the quiet moments of peace.

I was made to walk boldly,
to smile without hesitation,
to open my arms to love
without bracing for the fall.

I was made for **restoration.**
For **healing** that is not just skin-deep
but soul-deep.

And that is exactly what He is doing—
taking these **broken pieces**,
lifting me from the ashes,
and making me **whole again.**

Decades Later, It Still Hurts

They say time heals.
But they never tell you that time
can also hold pain in its hands,
tucking it into the corners of your body
like it never left.

Decades later, I hear a name,
a sound, a scent,
and suddenly, I am back there.

The room.
The hands.
The moment I wish I could erase.

They say to let it go,
but I do not know how to let go
of something that still has its claws in me.

I have carried this silence
longer than I should have,
longer than anyone should have to.

And yet—

I was never truly alone.

Because on the nights when my voice failed me,
when the weight of this past life
pressed into my ribs like a curse,
when I felt forgotten, discarded, ruined—

He was there.

Not just watching,
not just waiting—
but holding me up,
keeping me from falling into the abyss.

And if He held me then,
if He walked through fire with me then,
He will walk me out of it, too.

Legacy

I do not wish to be remembered
for the pain I endured,
for the battles I fought,
or for the scars left behind.

I wish to be remembered
for how I rose,
for how I turned my pain into purpose,
for the love I gave,
and for the strength I left behind
in those who walk after me.

Let my legacy be courage.
Let my name be a whisper of resilience.
Let my life be proof
that even the broken
can build something unshakable.

Reflection & Journaling

What legacy do you want to leave behind?

_____

_____

_____

_____

What does full restoration look like for you?

_____

_____

_____

_____

Acknowledgments

No book is ever written alone, and *The War She Won* is no exception. This collection would not exist without the support, encouragement, and prayers of so many.

To those who have walked beside me on this journey—whether through the darkest valleys or in the moments of rising—I am forever grateful. Your love, your strength, and your unwavering belief in me have helped shape this book in ways I could never put into words.

To every survivor who has ever felt unheard, unseen, or forgotten—this book was written with you in mind. Your courage, your resilience, and your unshakable spirit inspire me daily. May these pages remind you that your story matters, your voice deserves to be heard, and your healing is possible.

To my family and closest friends, thank you for lifting me up in ways that I will never be able to repay. Thank you for your patience, your faith, and your endless encouragement.

To every reader holding this book in your hands—thank you. Thank you for allowing these words to be part of your journey, for finding strength in these pages, and for walking this road with me.

And above all, to God—my healer, my refuge, and my source of unshaken strength. Every word in this book is a reflection of Your grace, and every victory is because of You.

With gratitude and love,

Isabel Barrett

Survivor Resources & Organizations

1. Crisis Hotlines (U.S. & International)
- National Sexual Assault Hotline (RAINN): 1-800-656-HOPE (4673) | www.rainn.org
- National Domestic Violence Hotline: 1-800-799-SAFE (7233) | www.thehotline.org
- Crisis Text Line (Text HOME to 741741)
- International Resources (For UK, Canada, Australia, etc.)

2. Christian-Focused Healing Organizations
- Hope for the Broken: www.hopeforthebroken.org (*Christian trauma recovery resources*)
- FaithTrust Institute: www.faithtrustinstitute.org (*For survivors of abuse in faith communities*)
- Celebrate Recovery: www.celebraterecovery.com (*Faith-based recovery program*)

3. Therapy & Self-Help Resources
- Find a Therapist (Psychology Today): www.psychologytoday.com
- EMDR Therapy for Trauma: www.emdria.org (*Specialized trauma therapy for PTSD healing*)

Afterword

The final page of a book is never truly the end—just as healing is never a destination, but a journey we continue to walk every day.

If you've made it this far, I want you to know something: *you are stronger than you think*. Every scar, every struggle, every silent battle you have fought has shaped you—not into someone broken, but into someone unbreakable.

This book was never meant to be just words on a page; it was meant to be a hand reaching out, a reminder that you are not alone. My prayer is that in these poems, you found pieces of your own story, echoes of your own resilience, and proof that even after the hardest seasons, beauty still rises from the ashes.

Wherever you are in your journey, know this—your war is not your identity. Your past is not your prison. You are worthy of healing, of peace, of joy. You are walking into a new chapter, one where your strength speaks louder than your scars and your future is not bound by your past.

Thank you for allowing me to walk this road with you. May you carry these words as a reminder of who you are: a survivor, a warrior, a woman unshaken.

With gratitude and strength,

Isabel Barrett

Anchored in Truth: Scriptures for Strength & Restoration

Healing and strength are not journeys we walk alone. Throughout every trial, every tear, and every triumph, God's Word offers us comfort, guidance, and unshakable truth. Below are carefully selected Scriptures that align with the themes you've encountered in this collection, reminding you that you are seen, known, and infinitely loved.

Survival & Strength

Isaiah 43:2

> *"When you pass through the waters, I will be with you; and when you pass through the rivers, they will not sweep over you. When you walk through the fire, you will not be burned."*

2 Corinthians 4:8-9

> *"We are hard pressed on every side, but not crushed; perplexed, but not in despair; persecuted, but not abandoned; struck down, but not destroyed."*

Healing & Restoration

Psalm 147:3

> *"He heals the brokenhearted and binds up their wounds."*

Joel 2:25

> *"I will restore to you the years that the swarming locust has eaten."*

Overcoming Fear & Anxiety

Philippians 4:6-7

> *"Do not be anxious about anything, but in every situation, by prayer and petition, with thanksgiving, present your requests to God. And the peace of God, which transcends all understanding, will guard your hearts and minds."*

2 Timothy 1:7

> *"For God has not given us a spirit of fear, but of power and of love and of a sound mind."*

Self-Worth & Unconditional Love

Psalm 139:14

> *"I praise you because I am fearfully and wonderfully made."*

Romans 8:38-39

> *"For I am convinced that neither death nor life, neither angels nor demons, neither the present nor the future...will be able to separate us from the love of God."*

Victory & New Beginnings

Isaiah 61:3

> *"To bestow on them a crown of beauty instead of ashes, the oil of joy instead of mourning, and a garment of praise instead of a spirit of despair."*

2 Corinthians 5:17

> *"Therefore, if anyone is in Christ, the new creation has come: The old has gone, the new is here!"*

Victory Over Our Enemies

Psalm 110:1

> *"The Lord said to my Lord, 'Sit at my right hand until I make your enemies a footstool for your feet.'"*

Refined Through Fire

1 Peter 1:7

> *"These trials will show that your faith is genuine. It is being tested as fire tests and purifies gold—though your faith is far more precious than mere gold."*

Jesus, the Light

John 8:12

> *"When Jesus spoke again to the people, he said, 'I am the light of the world. Whoever follows me will never walk in darkness, but will have the light of life.'"*

Freedom in Christ

John 8:36

> *"So if the Son sets you free, you will be free indeed."*

Galatians 5:1

> *"It is for freedom that Christ has set us free. Stand firm, then, and do not let yourselves be burdened again by a yoke of slavery.*

www.ingramcontent.com/pod-product-compliance
Lightning Source LLC
Chambersburg PA
CBHW031443040426
42444CB00007B/945